Sunflowers in Your Eyes

poetry from:
ETHEL IRENE KWABATO
BLESSING MUSARIRI
FUNGAI RUFARO MACHIRORI
JOICE SHERENI

MENNA ELFYN (ed)

Cinnamon Press
Independent Innovative International

Published by Cinnamon Press
Meirion House
Glan yr afon
Tanygrisiau
Blaenau Ffestiniog
Gwynedd
LL41 3SU
www.cinnamonpress.com

The rights of Fungai Rufaro Machirori, Blessing Musariri, Joice Shereni and Ethel Irene Kwabato to be identified as authors of this work has been asserted by them in accordance with the Copyright, Designs and Patent Act, 1988. Copyright © 2010
ISBN: 978-1-907090-13-4
British Library Cataloguing in Publication Data. A CIP record for this book can be obtained from the British Library.

Designed and typeset in Palatino by Cinnamon Press. Cover design by Mike Fortune-Wood from original artwork *'Sunflowers'* by Colleen Coombe, agency dreasmstime.com
Printed in Poland.

The editor's royalties from this publication are donated to the Women's Poetry Alliance, Zimbabwe and 'Slum Cinema', a voluntary initiative which seeks to empower disadvantaged communities through multi-media work.
Cinnamon Press is represented in the UK by Inpress Ltd www.inpressbooks.co.uk and in Wales by the Welsh Books Council www.cllc.org.uk.
The publisher acknowledges the financial assistance of the Welsh Books Council

Contents

Ethel Irene Kwabato

Fungai Rufaro Machirori

Joice Shereni

Blessing Musariri

Foreword

In poetry, we talk a great deal about two opposing forces—the sense of 'urgency' and the realisation that a poem has its own sense of ' time'. Here, in this collection those two very different concepts are inherent in the work of four accomplished women poets from Zimbabwe. These voices are much needed, conveying a world made magnificent in its humanity. These voices sing of an unquenchable spirit against the backdrop of convention and expectation. Their poems also display the canniness of place and in Olson's words 'a tracking of earth in time.'

I came across the women writers featured in this exciting new anthology in 2002, when the British Council sponsored an innovative project pioneered by Graham Mort, an on-line mentoring project which enabled some writers from the whole continent of Africa (almost), to be linked to established writers in the UK. I was lucky enough to be one of those mentors, and managed through the course of two years to be in touch with what was then termed 'emerging writers'. Today, many of those writers have fully emerged and are in fact, steadily making an impact on the literary world, winning prizes and gaining worldwide recognition.

When I visited Zimbabwe in 2004, to conduct workshops, I was more than impressed by the tenacity of the writers, as well as moved by their commitment to writing as a necessary activity. I met many gifted people whose work deserved a wider readership and yet, the opportunities of publishing seemed at that time remote. The women writers especially seemed to be faced with the extra task of raising families (extended to the children of siblings in many cases), as well as wanting to follow their need and hunger to write.

I hope this book goes some way in redressing this imbalance, with writers who have indeed gained recognition in their own lands gaining also that necessary wider readership. Those who view the adage of the seventies that the 'personal is political' as a redundant statement may well change their minds after reading these poems. Here the fusion of political and personal is imperative. If the writing seems at times to be raw and direct, one must be mindful of an oral tradition which is brimful of incantation and invective. Theirs is a poetry deeply rooted in the spoken word where passion and profundity come in equal measures. There are poems too in this collection which display restraint and irony, be their tone sombre or humorous.

Blessing Musariri coined a term which embodies all the poets in this collection. They share a 'humbling intensity' and Blessing's assured poems manage to elucidate that emotion. Ethel Kabwato's terse poems voice a restlessness at the existing order with irony and wit. Fungai Rufaro Machirori's quirky outpourings splash across the page with vivid solicitude whereas Joice Shereni's poems intertwine love and loss of a personal nature, so much so that we feel ourselves eavesdropping on her and her loved one. These writers never look away but demand our admiration for their sheer vitality and verve. They show us a world that is worth believing in, a world where women still reaching into the sky, which are, like these poets as tall as their desires and as bold as their stems.

Menna Elfyn

Sunflowers in Your Eyes

Ethel Irene Kabwato

Ethel Irene Kabwato was born in Mutare, Zimbabwe into a creative family and has won many prizes for her prose and poetry. Trained as a teacher, she holds a Bachelors of Arts degree in Media Studies with the Zimbabwe Open University. A founding member of the Zimbabwe Women Writers Project she participated in the Crossing Borders Project. She has been invited to read her work at institutions such as Rhodes University and University of Witwatersrand, South Africa on the occasion of the World-Wide Reading for media freedom in Zimbabwe, 2007. She was also a guest of 'Cinema without Borders 'at the Amnesty International Film Festival, Amsterdam. Currently, she is working on a project called Slum Cinema, a voluntary initiative which seeks to empower disadvantaged communities through multi-media work. Her inspiration is derived from her two daughters, Nadia and Wynona.

Amsterdam 2008

I carry with me
the African sun
across oceans
canals
rivers
lanes
I bring the sunshine
to a land of rainbows
and soft rains.
she welcomes me
this rare beauty
at Plantage Middenlaan
her warm embrace
enveloping me;
one who brings
the warmth
of the African sun
to faraway lands.

Junior's Morphine

Dear Sarah

While you queue
for mealie meal
and sugar, struggle
to get morphine
for your bed ridden son,
as you run away
from police brutality
and watch from afar
the burning hut
that was once home,
I stand vigil
after long hours
at the old people's home
in Bristol,
while your husband cuddles
my bosom
dreaming away the hours
…and the nightmare
of missing the route 41
tram for a shift
at the mental hospital,
I read another *sms*
from you,
desperate—
this time
Junior's morphine please,
no medicines in hospitals—
urgent.

I delete the message
before he wakes up,
to another shift which awaits him

and you wait,
for a reply that will never come,

Yours
Hagar.

Burial of an activist

They buried him today
lips and tongue
cut out
as if to silence
him
even in death.

Hate

So consuming
like uncontrolled
veld fire.

The Painting

Show me that painting
again
of happy children
playing.

Freedom

I thought you would give me
a little of your time,
time to let me know you,
and hold you.
time to carry me with you
when I cannot lift
my feet,
my voice,
my hands,
again.

give me time, freedom
time to get to know you,
so I can rewrite history.

National Hero Status

They conferred
national hero status
on him,
after long hours
of debate
and consultations.
over steaming cups
of rich creamy coffee
and imported chocolate
cookies;
they conferred
hero status
on a man
they all swore
they never knew
or met
At Mgagao, Chimoio,
or Nyadzonia.

Land

These grains of earth
in my hands
sift through
my peasant fingers,
as I wait
for rains
from the gods
and fertilizer
and seed
from those
above us
who promised
us the land
*when the elections
are over.*

Independence Day

We celebrate again—
though prematurely,
our independence,
not from the colonial masters
but from those
of our own skin:
the sons and daughters
of the soil,
who hold the nation
to ransom.

Reminiscences

This is the place
we once called home—
the place where we danced
during the full moon
and played hide and seek
behind the boulders
at the chief's homestead.
we called this place home
when the rivers were
still flowing in the summer,
and we would sing
and shout to the wind,
to give us good men,
but the wind carried
our voices
with it
and gave us tight-fisted men
whose cruelty we now see
in the eyes
of the nameless children we hold
in our unempowered hands:
the products
of a man made tragedy
that is haunting us.

From mother to son 1

This a black day
for you, son,
the day you wish
you could bury
your head in the sand.
I watched you
when you thought
I wasn't looking,
hiding the ruling party's regalia
—the black and white bandana
and the green t-shirt
with the Zimbabwe ruins
motif.
Son, the oversized
black militia boots
are under your single bed
—blood stained.
maybe they will come
for you
at night
or during the day
for everyone to see,
because they remember
the torture
of their loved ones
—the endless chant
of your slogans
—the chickens
you took from them
and the young girls
at the base
whose breasts you fondled.

From mother to son 2

They picked you up
that night in June
as the neighbours
watched from the windows
across the street.
I groped in the dark,
to get that flaming red jersey
that would keep you warm
wherever they took you
that cold night,
before the elections,
when I knew
I was seeing you
for the last time.

The Journey

We journey through strange lands
you and I,
our voices blending into one.
a reflection of the rape of the land
we once called home.
Our hearts belonged there—
now they are coated in purple
the colour of death,
we have turned our backs
on the land that has nurtured us.

When we had a voice
we used to sing
as we tilled the land,
the fresh smell of cow dung
still haunts us.
the ghosts of the farmers
whose horses still neigh
at night,
in the village cemetery.
follow us
across the borders.

We have walked away
from the hills and boulders,
from the rivers and the mountains,
from the sound of the bell
at Mount Carmel mission.
From the iron bird
and its flight:
as it swooped on us
in our white cotton socks
of virginity.

Where we have come from—
we have left women
who can no longer walk
away;
women who can no longer look
away in shame
when girls are raped;
women who now stand in defiance
against the iron bird,
whose presence
in the hills
reigns another era—
(the rape of the land.)

The Hunter

He left home
laden with promises,
a new arrival
in a foreign land,
a hunter on fabled streets
paved with gold.
a shepherd
feeding his flock
in absentia.

The hunter became the hunted
as back home
the clan demanded Forex
and the chefs promised Homelink,
to link him with his Forex-orphaned children,
prematurely abandoned,
disillusioned,
trapped.

He became a second-class citizen
as the authorities
demanded the papers.

Now the hunter
arms himself with a cell phone
like a good shepherd
with his rod and stuff
as he yearns for the dawn
while his Forex orphans,

sleep and wait.

Birthdays

June is the month
when the girls
would paint the town red.
June is the month
when he
would bring
a cake home.
June is the month
when he
would sit back
and smile—
their laughter
warming his heart.
They are all gone now—
to distant shores
and into the hungry earth.

Now he visits them
every year in June
a dozen roses in hand
one for each of the children
who used to paint the town red.

Women's Day

I've seen you travel
the same road over the years,
I've watched you pick up
the broken threads of your life,
I've heard you sing
about the scars that you bear,
but you have not faltered.
I stand here and wait
for the sound
of the African drum,
whose silence
evokes a kaleidoscope of emotions
the haunting stillness
of dreams.
yet to be realised
I've watched you dance
to the silent drum
but the sores on your feet
are too heavy to take you through
to the last dance.
when you walk that same road again,
remember to take my heart with you
(because ours is a tie
that binds.)

Beauty Parlour

She was here again
—the mistress
as she talked about
her flat in the avenues.
as I bent for the pedicure
she slouched in her chair
and shouted for another wig
the latest one from Nigeria
but even the latest wasn't good enough:
It wasn't 100% human.
she wanted one made from
the hair of Russian women prisoners.
we listened as she closed her eyes
and continued…
the MAZDA 6
was now a kid's toy
On Samora Machel Avenue,
perhaps the x5
would do?
we learnt of Ferragano,
Stoned Cherry, Gucci,
Maxamara and Dior.
The names were beautiful
and yet to her nothing was perfect,
except of course, the mineral water.
When her cell phone rang
she purred on about London
and how she missed it.
she talked of Durban
And the Hummer they had to clear.
she said she hated
Berlin in winter
but, who could resist
the magic of Cape Town?

It was all lily-white,
a safe haven for the rich,
an Eden for the newly weds
and everyone who mattered
went there, anyway.

Her beauty restored
she stood up
red lips pouting,
car keys jingling.
gracefully, she left
leaving us without a tip.

We looked at each other.
What could she do?
Her lover, the minister
was still on remand.

The Strike

I've written to tell you
that they called off the strike.
it really doesn't matter who they are
you and I will never know,
neither will the empty stares
of the children
we teach.
We safely retire
and hang our jackets on the hook,
our chapped hands
dipped in empty boxes of brittle chalk,
our voices
once loud and passionate,
now a distant whisper,
as we teach them
about the revolution that never was.

Fungai Rufaro Machirori

Fungai Rufaro Machirori was born in Bulawayo, Zimbabwe in 1984. Her names 'Fungai' and 'Rufaro 'to think' and 'happiness' respectively in the Shona language express what she too strives for in life. As a poet she was chosen as one of 12 participants in the 'Crossing Borders' programme. In 2007, she was recognised with the Africa-wide award in excellence, in strategic communication on HIV and AIDS. She has also won national short-story and script writing competitions. Apart from being a poet and short-story writer, she is also a journalist, researcher and blogger. At the moment, she is working on her first novel as well as continuing with her professional path into international development with specific focus on gender issues.

I am not ketchup

I am not ketchup,
To be had on the side,
Along with a main course,
Poured somewhere on the edge of a plate,
Only to be called to use
If the meat tastes bland,
Or the gravy runs short,
Or the veggies need masking
from their insipidity.

I am not a condiment
To be smothered mercilessly onto a platter of food,
Oozing garishly and tactlessly
where I need not be:
For where I need be
Is deep within the wafting aroma
Of my own flavours
Distinct and complete,
Calling to attention those with senses trained in
the appreciation of
the finer things in life.

Born Free

I know not the oppression
of whips flicking flecks of flesh from taut caramelled backs
burnt summer black and split with scarlet
streams of pain;
no, I will not deceive you with lines of things
I do not know
but through commentaries of history I find in books
I read half-awake
to get a credit for an O' Level pass;
forgive my ignorance of the past, for you see,
I was born free
you speak endlessly on my hands-free
and dream away African ancestry,
and speak my mind—
decolonised, my thoughts strain to find a connection
to your wars and foes
as I sit in your libraries trying to trace the threads that string
my beads of blood to the hangman's noose that choked *your* dreams;
I care not for your oppression,
or your oppressor,
Your state of emergency,
or your emergence from the state,
I know not the past because
I care not,
want not,
need not.

Day's Break

Everything is innocent at birth;
Even a new day descending
over a sleeping world,
with its slow whisper of first breath,
its fast-changing hues of new life that morph the vague darkness
into the softness of an artist's pastels.

At dawn, the sky is a stainless canvas
On which we can draw our day's dreams and destinies,
At daybreak, the voices of doubt and unbelonging are still asleep,
far too tired from yesterday's endless taunts and jeers,
And all we hear are the chirps and squawks of the early birds—
no sin, no lies,
nothing yet to deny or despise,
Just the sunrise
Singeing the skies
With a refiner's fire
Rekindling a people's desires.

Manifestation

Be strong! she croaks
in the wiry thread of her voice,
Her eyes bulging from their sockets,
Criss-crossed with scarlet tributaries,
Her fingers creased and gnarled like talons trained
in snatching prey from the prowler's peril.

Be strong!
I echo the words back to myself in a whisper.
Who am I to drink of the sap of strength's sturdy stems?
I ask myself
Who am I to...?

You are, she interrupts with a sway of her head
of beaded dreadlocks,
The manifestation of worlds and wars, love and heat,
surrender and seasons.
You are compassion and spite,
strife and ceaselessness,
you are a force within god's winds,
and you are worth each story,
each page of ink
each word,
written in history,
now
manifested
by your presence.

ATM (Attempt To Move-on)

Deep within my love-box,
your name rattles back and forth
like the last dime that won't fall through the slim slit
of a little girl's piggybank;

Yours is the cheque that won't clear and can't be cashed,
the balance that remains once all else has been transacted
and transferred;
the reserves that keep my account from falling into arrears.

With my ATM card in hand,
I've often thought of releasing the last traces of you
from my stores,
But with each try,
I fail to punch that simple secret six letter pin code
U-N-L-O-V-E
That would release you from my burdened chest.

I Am

I am a composition
of words, full stops and commas of blood clotted through
the paragraphs of nerves that write my story
on pages of flesh and bone.
My skin's the thin envelope
that seals this letter of lyrics
written, unread, unspoken—
address unknown
travelling unopened
to your doorstep
to unwrap and read
me into life.

Tears will not cure

I don't cry anymore—
for as I lie there mourning
the death of yesterday,
this empire of changing tide
still holds fast to its promises
still beats, erupts and overflows
with a molten myriad of hopes,
and all our brittle dreams.

As I surrender—voiceless and powerless
in opposition to the hours fading—
there's still a crown life
with blinding light,
that halos this undeserving world,
and I must package my sorrows
and fall back into line
with a band of soldiers
whose fears are camouflaged
not by pride
but the pursuit of freedom.

Woman

No man is worth fear or fighting,
or faithlessness.
no man is worth the loss of self
and certainty.
No man is worth tears,
shed for
his callousness;
his thoughtlessness.
No man is worth submission
to powerlessness
and silence,
or idle dreams dreamt on pillows of
weightless promises,
for love, if true, seeks
your soul's innermost celebration
and outward manifestation
of
being
beautifully
woman.

Loved out

I don't want to meet the impostor
called Love
who'll rap at the tender door of my heart,
and force his way through
to the inner rooms of my being,
invading my throne
to crown himself
king.

Kingless—I'd rather wrap cold chains and iron locks
around the throbbing core of me
and watch and let my fetters grate and rust and cool
my blood
as i create a boundary,
a beautiless sight
that love might walk past
without invading,
without undoing the deliberate works of a wary soul
trained in fear and pain.

Untitled

My monthly contract with nature;
signed indefinitely,
is to flow with waves of fertility
like a crimson Nile
gushing with the promise of new life.

And yet if I speak of this tide
erupting secretly from my shores,
you flinch and take offense
at my celebration
of self,
calling my speech
vulgar and
unclean;
for you will accept bloodshed from battles,
and raw wounds from street fights,
but nothing of my body's dance
and ebbs and flows
to its own set rhythm;
you accept my femininity in the curve of my hips and
the soft fullness of my breasts,
but not in my menstrual mysteries
padded and
plugged and
plunged into darkness
to conceal the depths of
my richness.

Tea Break

Staring out the window as the people popple
and froth over the paved streets,
she creates a vortex in her creamy coffee,
her piston-arm whirling a teaspoon that scrapes
and tingles against the ceramic cup she's forgetting
to drink from,
instead she wishes she could taste the crowd's
different blends
and percolate through their thoughts
as she creates more forceful currents of steam
escaping
blandly, idly
from her mind.

The story of she

Each day, she awakens early to disturb
the sleeping soils from their slumber,
scraping and raking raw rows into the silent plains,
hunched low, she works near enough to smell the
secrets and listen to the lures of the earth.
But as she carries out her chore,
she somehow loses herself to thoughts of death,
and how this calamity, this chaos and coarseness is
her only source of calm from a life that ceaselessly
makes demands,
and never concessions with her soul;

desires she once had numb and harden
like the callous palms she uses to hold her hoe and
dig and clash with the earth
in pursuit of life;
where she finds none for herself.

In the silence all she hears is her breath, quickening;
and her heart pacing through her thoughts,
wishing it would stumble upon one of her darkest
imaginings and throb its last beat in deathly shock:
What is there to live for?
She asks without words,
Her muscles tensing and flexing to bring order
to the earth that yields nothing for her own dreams.

The sweat beads collect and then dribble down her face,
salty like her tears and strife.
Soon, she knows the sun will peer through the veil
of her sorrows,
and beat cruelly on her face,
and the earth, now dark and dreamy, will reveal again its
shades of scarlet
like the blood she wishes would seep
out of her veins and collect
in the hands of God.

Tribute

If I could
store your essence
in a vial
I could wear
close to my heart,
I would,
because like a charm,
or enchanting fragrance,
You are
the enticement
that keeps me throbbing
and pulsing with
possibility.

You are more than Spirit or Soul,
flesh or form—
You are the jasmine blooming in my garden of thought,
the lavender seeping through my skin,
and the tiger lily singeing the dark corners of my heart;
and I carry you
like a treasure
buried in the depths of my existence,
emanating through the glow in my eyes
and the slow arch of my smile.

You are indelible
for you have dared tread
the stony pathway to my being
and taken refuge there in my simple space,
leaving feet, hands and heart,
embedded
engraved
upon each tile
that paves my onward journey.

I

I exist—
away from the throbbing cords,
and silent seed pods where the
unborn
grow flesh that must harden.

I exist—
where tears dry,
where chains are broken and molten
in the raging fire of freedom,
where hope is the glistening machete we carry as
defence
against our planet.

I exist,
I breathe in life,
I am.

Right and wrong

Right words, wrong voice,
right daydream, wrong day,
right touch, wrong hands,
right kiss, wrong lips,
right dreams, wrong pillow,
right soul, wrong flesh,
write words to forget the wrong one.

Cashless Society

Smoking halos of zeros
ascend from the torched pile of countless notes
we use now to kindle tinder memories
of being once
meaningless millionaires,
fanning a myriad layers of
false wealth at the hot hissing coals of
poverty's hell,
whose thick air chokes and gropes at our hope once more
as we spit drawn slugs of sputum
onto the mounds of ash that begin to gather at our feet.
our expired creation cremated
to barren wastes of lies and dust
through which we burrow our stung toes,
asphyxiating, grating at the mad heat of uncertainty
uncertain
of sure ground in which to plant our dreams
combusting
to budless seed.

She

She catches my thoughts—
they halt.

skin dusky, smooth
like a greying sunset,
eyes precisely preened, pristine
lined with perfect strokes of ebony,
lips rich with the sweetness of African mahogany;
dark hair she's swept down her face—
thick and obedient to her command.

Does she know it
and ponder it as she sits there on her rickety throne,
that she makes men stutter
and women quiver in awe?
Nubian princess on this rainy evening,
meets the lopsided pauper that is me,
ashamed but never grudging,
as once more, our kombi* rattles and creaks—
she is the most beautiful woman I've ever seen.

Sixty Sheets

I hope she arrived home safely,
that old woman with her baby toes
peeping out of her black tennis shoes
worn from treading the relentless tar and dust
of Harare's streets;
that old woman who stopped me along my way,
resting her dirty plastic sack along the road
to ask if I'd buy some avocados from it
so she could make enough money for fare to Highfield.
I'm desperate, my child, she pleaded,
The deep lines of despair in her withered face coming together
to draw a picture of her dejection:
Three trillion dollars, all she asked for—
sixty sheets of notes
that would ferry her tired soul home in a rickety ride
where, for a few minutes, she might cast away her woes;
I watched her,
that burdensome sack of avocados trailing her on her back,
soiling her white dress.
A woman her age should not have to work so hard,
should not have to cup her palms together in gratitude
for so little as sixty sheets
of worthlessness.

Joice Shereni

Joice Shereni was born in 1976 and is the second child in a family of six. She works as a Senior Buyer, in Triangle, a small town in the lowveld. A single mother of two children Tanaka and Daniel, she finds inspiration is all that is around her and writing empowers her to shed light on her understanding of the world. She also gains strength from her religious belief and a verse she holds dear is Micah 7, verse 8 'Rejoice not against me O mine enemy when I fall, I shall arise. When I sit in darkness the Lord shall be a light unto me.' She also writes 'because writing allows me to be who I am meant to be.'

Matrimony

While I hide,
turn my face from you
and hurt,
I want to reach out to you
because you
understood me once;
the gap between us
threatens the hope
that I could have been,
may still be to you
more than I am
yet you do not reach
out to me as before,
because although I hurt
I am still
the mother of your children
and will always be
your best friend,
your wife.

Pity

Would you like
to prod me
see if I flinch?
Open me,
see what I am made of.
Do I bleed
should you cut me?
Will I run and hide
should you hunt me?
Will you not
be merciful
and let me heal
from wounds
that bleed
from past battles?

Destiny

Should I let myself
need you?
must I be honest
and admit to myself
what you mean to me?

I do not want
to depend on you
for my happiness
because
in accepting your reality
I'm losing control.

Rejection

The night is dark and lonely
and my heart is heavy,
my eyelids slowly dimmer
slowly framing my cheeks;
the heavy dew of sadness
rolling
condensing in my upturned palms.

My eyes seek your face in darkness
trying to draw comfort from you,
wanting to reach out, touch you,
hold that familiar hand.
As my hand grazes yours
our eyes locking,
you shrink back from my touch,
the heavy words tumbling out,
making the air around us hot,
the radiation of your anger.
You turn around and walk away
leaving me broken.

A forbidden clay pot
in the hands of
a naughty child
—unable to heat
without a feast for supper.

Hunters

It was not so much their words,
it was the way they looked at me,
(scrutinized me)
and tore me apart,
with their pity—
that left me
feeling naked,
ashamed,
until I wanted to
run
and hide myself
from their prying eyes.
I could taste their eagerness
to hunt me down
so I could be like them
waiting for some weak prey—
so I too, could taste
bitterness.

Husband

Why can you not...?
You,
the flesh I became.
Can you not see
how you tore apart
the walls around me
the partitions that
protect my private dreams
and left me
abandoned,
unprotected?
You should have been
my secret cave,
my hideout,
within these walls,
these partitions,
a guard at the door.

Why do you hurt me?
Bring down plasterboards
of words,
tear apart
demolish with actions.
can you not see
how you tear yourself too,
flesh of my flesh?

When the pain
of pounding walls becomes
unbearable...

Listen!
I am your wife
your friend
I cannot harm you.
Why not make me
your mirror
in a blue coloured room?
Our sky, our roof?
So I can show you
what mockery is
in the making.

Patches

Turn the pages
of my scrapbook,
look at me.
what I was
before,
what I
could have been.

Now,
see me, now
as I was then,
not what I am.
Do not see
my faded threads,
the wear and tear
of knotted hems.
Turn a blind eye
to my fall from grace;
it is merely one patch
on the eiderdown of my life,
a strand of me
that can be gathered
and quilted anew
with patches of life
this,
to give you
what I could have been—
(yet could not).

All I can offer you now,
is what I have:
Palpable patches,
that once were
sown in me.

Blessing Musariri

Blessing Musariri is an award-winning children's author who has published widely. Her publications include *Rufaro's Day* (Longman Zimbabwe 2000), *Going Home: A Tree's Story*, (Weaver Press, Zimbabwe, 2005) and *The Mystery of Rokodzi Mountain* (Hodder Education, UK). She has also been featured in various international anthologies and recently awarded a special prize in the Susie Smith Memorial Prize Competition, Oxfam with her work displayed on their website. Although she initially believed she would become a lawyer, she changed her mind after sitting and passing the English Bar Finals in 1997. She also holds a Masters in Diplomatic Studies from the University of Westminster.

To Polokwane and Back—
Conversations on the Highway

Baobab trees watch the road like old men waiting
for Jesus to come like a thief in the night.

We follow a shimmering strip that cows and donkeys cross
as if they are walking on water.

We cross the Old Bridge with no fear of drowning,
the sun has eaten the river ; left the sand astonished.

Dolomite hills stand out like baffled humpbacked whales
who have lost the sea, did they rise or did the earth fall away?

Do the trees know that while they stand here in stone,
they have left their brothers and sisters to be sacrificed
on the altar of dual carriageways—limbless stumps,
guarding *men at work*.

Somebody's goat is dancing in the middle of the road
making the cars stop and stare.
Where is the herd boy sleeping? He will wake
to find his animals keening for the foolish kid who dared and lost.

Daylight falls behind the city limits and we hide from night.
Tomorrow clouds will kiss the mountaintops and descend
to caress gun-grey metal snaking,
to clothe it in morning's mist of devotion.

Holding On

Everyone has moved on.
What were you doing standing still
in a shrinking city, dreaming of Christiana
and popcorn in the shape of animals from a machine
she has wheeled into the room while
you were dancing with Nombi to hip hop
on the radio?
You don't learn,
you keep losing because you dream
too much of winning and you do not see that
you're drowning—

Maybe, they keep you afloat,
your sisters,
and never tell you that you're
swimming against the current
and the scent of white lilies in a box, with an angel
untimely called to heaven—

I wish God had let us keep her—

pain from so long ago, uninvited,
sits with me as we watch you speak life into words,
believing in things you have yet to see,
drinking wine in the afternoon on weekdays and laughing
with friends, saying you are *the keeper of Indian girl's secrets*
and that is all you have in your pockets but they love you all the same.

Who has given you the right to be so happy with nothing in your head
but scribbled bits of paper—words on your mind,
silken threads of seductive horizons,
places only you will ever know.
But everyone has moved on,
you won't listen to what I say even though experience
has shown you the truth I speak, as hope fools time
and rhymes again. You clutch fistfuls of fancy—
smile and say—*Hold on sister, just keep holding on.*

Last Goodbye

The old neighbourhood has not stood well the ravages of time passing through the hands of careless tenants and owners who have died and left their children to fight amongst themselves as paint peels and walls collapse. The families are all gone and the houses are full of people whose trees fall into neighbours' yards with no apology or retrieval—broken branches of indifference.

There are holes in the streets into which blind men disappear and children can no longer run to the shops barefoot, without telling their mothers that they have found twenty cents in the tuft of grass that stops the gate from closing tightly shut. Do you remember that day? The hot tar, the long grass of the small field we cut across and the dust that clung to our feet as we threw that silver coin on the counter and called out for nigger balls—half a cent each—cheap sweets, dirty on our tongues.

The grass now swallows the black iron grill from where I used to swing and call you out to play. Strangers bask in the sun on your verandah on Sundays and don't call out 'Good morning' as I walk by. Where did your mother go while I was away? That day I came to see you and you had gone to your aunt's home in Highfields, we talked for hours—me, legs kicking from a low branch in your guava tree while she snipped and tugged at weeds in her bed of magnolias. She said I was really her friend, not yours, and I was pleased. Why did your father walk out after all those years, without a word?

The spirit that once was the neighbourhood now resides in the one place that stands untouched by the slow death of all we knew. Here my mother still kneels and praises God for all she has lost and found. I still hear my aunt's voice above all the others in the choir, at the front, even though she now sings from Heaven. There are those here who seek deliverance from the tortures of familial spirits, those who search for peace and guidance, and me. We were here the last time I saw you—the throbbing of the beating drums in my heart, the spattering rhythm of the shaking gourds and the ululation as everyone stood up to sing.

Mitu's Spice Tour

It's raining, wet and muddy. Stop one—Hamida's on the phone.
Jackfruit tastes like pineapple mixed with banana,
dorian is a fruit that tastes like heaven but smells like hell;
not allowed in many places.
Use henna leaves to make the dye.

Stop two—Celia's lost a shoe in squelching mud.
Soursop, also known as elephant apple
gives hair gel if you soak the seeds.
The coconut plantation is owned by the government;
there are three types of palm.
The crooked one was struck by lightning.

Stop three—a lady is bitten by something on wings.
To make red dye take annatto seeds,
related to the litchi, makes natural lipstick.
Cardamom and vanilla need the shade.
Papaya wine makes you blind for a while,
with seventy-one percent alcohol—very bad hangover.

Stop four—in single file we are baking in the sun.
Cloves cure diarrhoea and stomach-ache,
the neem is very bitter but better than malaria parasite.
Boil bark or leaves and drink tea for seven days.
Cures up to forty ailments.

Last stop—don't feel so good.
Walked too much, drank too little, didn't have a hat;
but, thank you ladies and gentlemen, for your kind attention,

lunch is served shortly on the bus.

Breaking News

This morning on the news, a child was found
wrapped in plastic bags in a sewer. The president
of a country somewhere far away from us was shot
by his bodyguard, rival ethnic groups are burning
each other's homes to the ground, the military has
imposed a curfew. In a village on some southern latitude
a man has hacked his wife to death and eighty succumb
to a mysterious fever. A teenage boy kills twenty classmates,
takes a bullet to his head and leaves no explanation,
only that he was quiet and kept mostly to himself. The New Party
spokesman says violence is not acceptable but you are
either with us or against us, there is no hallow ground.
Air strikes are rife in the Middle-east, thousands flee for life
leaving many dead and dying. This morning on the news,
a woman throws a television from a sixth floor window,
no passersby were injured—good news indeed,
in fact this is no news at all.

Related

I
I am sponsored by…

The Kenyan sandal-maker says: my shoes are not fragile and un-enduring. It is you who walks without care. If you daydream in the streets you will not see the pavement rise up to meet you in places where concrete slabs have parted ways—miniscule mountains, of consequence only to unwary toes. Sleepwalker you have stumbled more than once and you speak of it with wonder that, leather parts from leather, thrusting hot tar underneath your feet with so little warning. Dream on dreamer, but do not walk while sleeping.

II
In the city of kings…

He stands up front and tells the story of his life. He knows that somewhere in the crowd there is someone who needs to hear it. Someone will laugh, or cry. He speaks from the heart because when the mind takes over there'll be nothing left to say. It's about the children; saving hopes and dreams from the oppression of urban age where they disappear into hoods and sneakers, powerful in posturing, respected on demand. He stands to break internal silence.

III
The space in between...

Daytime flights are dangerous because you see the place you might land should you chance to fall. Here among rolling clouds my thoughts meander—this is as close to snow as I'll get today, as close to you—standing in the foyer, laughing about how your father bought you an Easter egg for your birthday. A glass of wine with lunch has aroused my fancy—touching cool glass as if I have touched your face. High in this blue sky, in nothing else but sky, I am further than I have ever been from you.

IV
Kalahari desert dreams

People are eating geckos in my dream. In the day, they speak in languages I don't understand so I sip cups of tea and nibble on small squares of pink cake—surprisingly delicious. The sun beats the rhythm of a dry season and behind sunglasses, beneath hats and caps and umbrellas, we melt. Amid different tongues and strange tastes, the lights go out at four a.m and I find myself in darkness.

Popular Fiction

she's looking for love in a CLK,
silver like a bullet straight to my heart,
she said,
that's what i want ,   she smears her lips
orange flame and pouts,   yes
i would be somebody then,   a yard
bigger than your fields of maize in
tribal trustlands and walls like those of Jericho
behind which i, sleek and spoiled, will hide
from these narrow streets   endless acceptance
of mediocrity,   she strokes a rough palm
over stretched denim and winds her waist to a silent tune
this body has a future you know—two kids no more,
she smiles,
repairs to follow,   yes
would you ask me to sweep your muddy floors then,
offer me day-old sadza and sugar bean stew hmm?
i would laugh in your face,
she draws on some eyebrows in black pencil
lines her eyes   shakes
a mane of sixty thousand dollar hair
from union street flea market,   oh yes
baby-girl's got a dream,   silver like a bullet
a crown on this pretty head   me—ghetto queen

Checking In

I was yours for a time,
to do with as you pleased,
believing in the fable of L O V E,
and the story of you captured my attention,
kept me hooked.
Convinced me that in your reality
you and me was we two,
together equals us and
I became a reflection of the me
I left enraptured at the place
where we first met and
I misread the signs that Fate
laid out to mark the path and you,
you with sunflowers in your eyes
and your smile full of light and promise.
You, with your hands that held me
as if they beheld all that was precious
in this world and rare
and you cherished the hours,
the days, the weeks turned into months,
back into the day we stood under harsh electric lights
and said goodbye,
me, thinking it was only for a while
and you, knowing the time had come
when you were no longer mine,
to do with as I pleased, to L O V E,
even as you unhooked from the story of me
and told them at the check-in counter
that you had no excess baggage.

Night Spells

My mother cannot sleep at night
someone has stolen her dreams
so that she does not see what she knows will be true
she
holds a shovel of glowing embers to the eaves
where an owl comes to roost and tells it
in the name of all that is holy to leave her thoughts to peace
in
her realm of sleeplessness
she hears sounds that do not belong to a house
in which she has lived for over fifty years
and she prays for sleep to come
but
sleep will not grace her mind
with its quiet whispers
and darkness
tries to wean her
from the light
fear
numbs fingers
that search for God
in rosary stones
from a mountain shrine in Rio
but
God will not be found
until walls re-appear
in the cool light
of near-dawn
and
the
long
night

lingers.

After Rain

Wild things are growing with lush abandon in ditches
fed by burst sewer pipes. They don't seem to mind the smell.
The soil is a decadent gateaux, the green is incandescent.
Weeds, purple and yellow masquerade and some, no flower at all,
made beautiful by sunlight.

Lamp-posts are headless giraffes confounded by concrete,
on moon-lit streets, impotent witness to frequent
muggings of women late home from work. No soft yellow guidance
back to gentler times.

The streets now own small countries, vassal states
often flooded after the rain, upon which cars may burst a tyre,
bend a rim or part with hubcaps after a sudden jolting
at point of immigration—no visas are required.